Babysitter's Backpack

Let's **PLAY!**

Awesome Activities
Every
BABYSITTER
Needs to Know

by Melissa Higgins

Consultant:
Lyn Horning
Assistant Director, Better Kid Care
Penn State University
University Park, Pennsylvania

CAPSTONE PRESS
a capstone imprint

Snap Books are published by Capstone Press,
1710 Roe Crest Drive, North Mankato, Minnesota 56003
www.capstonepub.com

Library of Congress Cataloging-in-Publication Data
Higgins, Melissa, 1953–
  Let's play : awesome activities every babysitter needs to know / by Melissa Higgins.
pages cm. — (Babysitter's backpack)
  Includes index.
ISBN 978-1-4914-0763-9 (library binding)
ISBN 978-1-4914-0767-7 (eBook pdf)
1. Babysitting—Juvenile literature. 2. Play—Juvenile literature. 3. Amusements—Juvenile
literature. I. Title.
  HQ769.5.H54 2015
  649'.10248—dc23
                          2014006644

Editorial Credits
Abby Colich, editor; Juliette Peters, designer; Tracy Cummins, media researcher;
Laura Manthe, production specialist

Photo Credits
Alamy: David Young-Wolff, 18; Capstone Press: Karon Dubke, 1 Bottom Right, 2 Bottom
Left, 5 Top, 9, 11, 12 Top, 13, 14, 16, 19 Top, 21 Top, 25 Bottom, 27 Top; iStockphotos: Jo
Unruh, 20, Metinkiyak, 8 Top, Yuri Arcurs, 7; Shutterstock: Africa Studio, 28 Middle
Right, Agorohov, 28 Bottom Right, Bogdan Ionescu, 28 Bottom Left, Denis Cristo, Cover,
design element, Denis Kuvaev, 1 Bottom Left, 4, Hugolacasse, design element, Maryna
Kulchytska, 2 Bottom Right, 23, Natykach Nataliia, 28 Top,Solphoto, 10, StockLite, 17 Top,
Tomasz Trojanowski, 15, Veerachai Viteeman, design element, ZouZou, 6

Printed in the United States of America in
North Mankato, Minnesota.
032014   008087CGF14

Page 4

Page 13

Table of Contents

Page 16   Page 23

CHAPTER 1

Play Is Fun and Important

Watching someone's children is a big responsibility. Babysitting is a business you need to take seriously. But that doesn't mean it can't be fun. In fact, play is good for you and for the children you babysit.

Why Play Is Good

Happy and busy children are more likely to behave, which will make your job easier. When the children you babysit are happy and behaving, you know you're doing a good job. Families will hire you again and refer you to other families.

What Should You Do quiz questions throughout will help you know if you're ready to be a great babysitter. You can look up the answers on page 29.

Different Ways to Play

Play is important for a child's growth and learning. There are different types of play. Each type helps children in meaningful ways.

- Active play, such as running, jumping, swinging, and dancing, helps children develop physically.
- Creative play, such as drawing, painting, making music, and make-believe, helps children use their imaginations.
- Thinking games, such as sorting, solving puzzles, counting, and learning rhymes, improve children's minds.
- Social play, such as team sports or taking turns on the playground, helps children learn to get along with others.
- Quiet play, such as reading or looking at books, playing with small table toys, or coloring, helps children calm down.

Doing activities with the children you babysit is a win for everyone. But before you set up that board game or twirl a jump rope, there are a few things you need to know.

CHAPTER 2

Before You Get Started

There are several things to keep in mind when planning activities. Safety always comes first. You should also know what parents will allow. Choose activities that are appropriate for the child's age. Being flexible and planning ahead will help you and the children stay safe and have fun.

What Should You Do?

The girl you're babysitting falls while riding her bike. She's crying. You should first ...

- **A** call 9-1-1.
- **B** check to make sure you and the child are in a safe place.
- **C** promise her a snack if she'll stop crying.
- **D** laugh at her for being clumsy.

Safety

Here are some tips for keeping everyone safe and happy during play:

- **Play with the children.** Don't just watch. It's not OK for you to start them on an activity and then go watch TV, do homework, or text your friends. Joining in gives you a chance to model good behavior. It may also help prevent behavior problems before they start.
- **Read all toy and game warnings and directions. Know how toys work and how to use them.** Check the ages recommended on the box or instructions. Only use toys or games that are appropriate for the child's age.
- **Make sure children under age 3** don't have access to objects they could swallow or choke on. If an object can fit through a cardboard paper towel tube, it's a choking hazard.
- **Put all risky toys out of reach of infants and toddlers.** These include toys with tears, loose buttons, broken parts, sharp points, long strings, and electronic toys that might cause burns.
- **Wash your hands before and after playing.**

Follow House Rules

Every family is different. One family may think it's fine for children to tap dance on the hardwood floors. Another family may frown on dancing entirely. If a parent doesn't tell you the rules up front, ask what they are. Here are some questions to ask when planning activities:

TV and Video Games: Can the children watch TV or play video games? Is there a time limit? Are there any programs, channels, or games that are off limits? How late can they watch or play?

Phone, Texting, and Computers: Are the children allowed to use cell phones? Are they allowed to text? Is it OK if they use a computer? If so, what computer activities are allowed?

Going Outside: Can you take the children outside? If so, do they need to stay in the yard, or can you take them for a walk? If so, how far are you allowed to go?

Active Play: Are children allowed to be rowdy and run around? Or do parents want them to play calmly and quietly?

You may have a special activity in mind that's not covered by any of these house rules. Always get a parent's permission first.

Choose Appropriate Activities

As children grow, their interests and abilities change. For example, a 1-year-old boy is too young to play Monopoly. And his 10-year-old brother doesn't want to play peek-a-boo. Choosing the right activities for the age of the child helps keep everyone safe. Age-appropriate activities that interest the child help prevent behavior problems by keeping him or her from becoming frustrated or bored.

What Should You Do?

You've started a craft. The girl you're babysitting yells, "This is stupid!" and walks away. You should ...

A ask the child what she would like to play.
B continue the craft on your own, hoping the child will see how much fun you're having.
C scold the child for being rude.
D give up doing any activities and go watch TV.

Be Flexible

Not all children enjoy the same things. Some children are more active than others. If a child doesn't want to play a certain game or activity, respect his or her wishes. Ask the child what he or she would like to play. Children also mature differently and reach stages of development at different times. If you're unsure about a child's abilities, ask parents what kinds of activities their child enjoys.

Plan Ahead

You will be babysitting two school-age children and have an amazing craft project in mind. Plan ahead by making a list of all the supplies you'll need. Does the family have these supplies? If not, who will buy them—you or the parents? If you provide the materials, do you expect to be repaid? Work out these details with a parent ahead of time.

Plan for how long a game or project will take. Will the parents only be gone an hour? Are the children going to bed soon? If so, don't start a craft or game that will take two hours. Also consider time to prepare and cleanup.

If you're babysitting more than one child, plan how you'll keep everyone occupied, especially if the children are different ages. If you do a single activity, be sure it is safe and appropriate for all children. Multiple activities are OK as long as you can safely watch every child at once. Be wise. Don't take on more than you or the kids can handle.

Clean Up After the Fun

When you're finished playing, return all toys and games where you found them. Put game pieces back neatly inside their boxes. The house should look as clean when you leave as it did when you arrived. Children can help you with cleaning up.

Activity Ideas for Infants and Toddlers

You have an awesome idea for an activity and it meets parents' approval. It's age appropriate and safe. Now it's time to play. Use your creativity and imagination.

Here are some examples of age-appropriate toys, games, and activities if you're running low on ideas.

Activities for Young Infants (Newborn to 6 Months)

Babies like to play on their own rather than with other children. They may only stay interested in an activity for a few minutes. So be patient and don't expect too much. Here are some toys and activities young infants may enjoy:

- simple toys with bright colors
- stuffed animals without buttons that could be a choking hazard
- teething toys
- rattles
- being held and rocked
- being cooed and sung to
- cloth or board books

Things to See and Hear

Babies like having different things to look at and listen to. Move the infant from one spot to another, giving him or her different things to look at. Even shadows from a window or the movement of a ceiling fan can be interesting to an infant. Talk, coo, or sing to the infant often. If it's a nice day, take the baby for a walk.

Activities for Older Infants
(6 Months to 1 Year)

Lots of development takes place between the ages of 6 months and 1 year. At 6 months babies are supporting their own heads. Soon after they're sitting, rolling, scooting, and crawling. At 9 to 12 months, babies are standing and some are taking their first steps. They may act shy with new people, but they like to watch and imitate others. Toys and activities older infants may enjoy include:

- large, soft blocks
- big stacking boxes or cups
- teething toys
- things that make noise, such as pots and pans, large bells, and squeaky toys
- throwing or dropping nonbreakable objects
- rolling a ball
- cloth books and simple picture books
- games like patty cake and peek-a-boo

Box of Fabric

Infants like to look and touch. Fill a small box with large squares of fabric of different colors and textures. Include fabrics that are soft, rough, silky, shiny, light, and dark. Pull a piece of fabric from the box and describe how it feels. Then give it to the baby to touch. Say, "This fabric feels soft. Would you like to touch the soft fabric?"

Activities for Toddlers
(1 to 3 Years)

Toddlers love to learn and do things for themselves. They also like to move around. What they don't love is to share, which means they don't make the best playmates. But they will play on their own beside other children. Some fun toys and activities for toddlers include:

- push and pull toys, like a toy wagon or shopping cart
- musical toys, like drums and shakers
- riding toys
- moving toys, like planes, cars, and trucks
- washable crayons, markers, and play dough
- toys that need arranging, like shape sorters and rings
- blocks for stacking and lining up to make roads
- dancing, rolling, jumping, and running
- singing songs
- imitating grown-ups and playing simple dress-up
- looking at picture books and being read to

Things in a Can

Toddlers can usually be entertained with simple games. Try cutting a hole in the lid of a large plastic tub. Make sure there are no sharp edges. Put the lid back on the container. Let the toddler drop craft sticks, clothespins, spoons, or other nonbreakable items inside. Be sure none of the objects are small enough to choke on. When finished, let the toddler dump the items out.

21

Activity Ideas for Preschoolers and School-Age Children

By age 3 children are becoming more coordinated. They can focus for longer periods of time and do more for themselves. The older the children are, the more creative you can be with your activities.

Activities for Preschoolers (3 to 5 Years)

Children between the ages of 3 and 5 start to interact with each other. They like to play simple games, but they may want to make up their own rules. Some toy and play ideas for preschoolers include:

- easy board games such as Chutes and Ladders and Candy Land
- pretend games such as playing school and shopping
- draping a sheet or blanket over a table or two chairs to make a tent
- stories read aloud
- jigsaw puzzles with big pieces
- hide-and-seek or tag
- riding wagons or tricycles
- playing musical instruments, such as drums, kazoos, or toy guitars
- playing with play dough or clay
- going on a treasure hunt
- making crafts, such as bookmarks, brown lunch bag puppets, collages, or necklaces made from cereal Os or dry macaroni

Treasure Hunt

A treasure hunt will challenge children and be fun at the same time. Make a map of the children's backyard. Hide a "treasure" somewhere in the yard. Mark an X on the map. The X can be the location of the treasure or another clue. The clue might read, "Walk 10 steps toward the fence. Hop 5 times and squawk like a chicken. Crawl under the slide. Climb over the rock. Look behind the tree trunk." Hide as many clues as you like.

Activities for School-Age Children (5 to 10 Years)

Rules are important to children who are ages 5 to 10. They understand teamwork, taking on roles, and having a leader. The activity ideas are endless for school-age children. Keep in mind that the abilities and attention span of a 5-year-old will be less than those of a 10-year-old. Here are a few game and play ideas:

- reading books
- drawing
- action dolls and fashion dolls
- board games such as checkers, Monopoly, Clue, and Sorry
- word games such as Scrabble and Boggle
- jigsaw puzzles
- putting on a play, puppet show, or talent show
- writing a story together
- outdoor activities, such as soccer, basketball, hopscotch, jump rope, riding bikes or scooters, or throwing a football, softball, or Frisbee
- making crafts with beads, yarn, paper, paint, clay, boxes, or other materials

Puppet Show

A puppet show is a fun activity that will let children be creative. Have the children help you write a script. Decorate socks or paper bags to create a puppet for each character. Use a tabletop or cardboard box as a stage. Practice your puppet voices. Put on a final performance for parents when they get home.

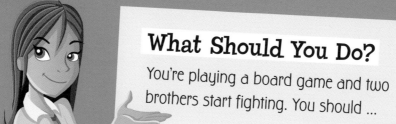

What Should You Do?

You're playing a board game and two brothers start fighting. You should ...

A punish the child who started the fight.

B get up and walk away.

C sit patiently and wait for the siblings to work out their own problems.

D stop playing and talk with the children.

What Should You Do?

You're stacking blocks with a 2-year-old. Her 5-year-old sister is jealous and wants your attention. You should ...

A play with the child who is the loudest.
B play with whichever child you like the best.
C tell the 5-year-old to wait her turn.
D try to give both children equal attention.

Activities for Different Age Groups

You're babysitting an infant, a 2-year-old, and an 8-year-old. You want an activity that's fun and appropriate for all three children. Here are a few ideas for all age groups.

- Walk around the neighborhood. Take a trip to the playground or a field trip to the library.
- Roll, bounce, or throw balls into a box or laundry basket.
- Play with blocks. Infants and toddlers can stack and knock them over. Preschool and school-age children can build more detailed structures. Remember to check the size of the blocks to make sure they are safe for use by infants and toddlers.
- Make homemade musical instruments and have a parade.
- Read aloud from a book. Young children may lose interest quickly if you aren't reading a book with pictures. Give younger children board books to look at as you read to older children.

Homemade Musical Instruments

There are lots of ways to make musical instruments with the kids you're babysitting. Partially fill empty plastic spice jars with beans, buttons, or beads. Glue on the lids to make a rattle. Turn a plastic tub or coffee can upside down to make a drum. Use a wooden spoon for a drumstick. Use two saucepan lids about the same size for banging cymbals. Make a guitar by cutting a hole in a shoebox lid. Tape the lid on the shoebox, stretch a few rubber bands across the hole, and strum the rubber band "strings."

Activities Tote Kit

It's a good idea to keep supplies ready so you can grab them on your way to any babysitting job. Keep items together in one place. A plastic box with a handle that securely fastens is a good choice. If you don't plan on being reimbursed for your supplies, don't spend too much money. The supplies should last through several babysitting jobs.

Some things you might want to include are:

- drawing paper (you can store paper items in folders or envelopes)
- crayons
- colored pencils
- sidewalk chalk
- glue stick
- old magazines for making collages
- safety scissors to use with preschool and school-age children
- play dough or other non-hardening clay stored in an airtight container
- blowing bubbles
- hand puppets
- a list of age-appropriate games and activities
- activity how-to descriptions

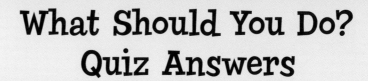

What Should You Do?
Quiz Answers

page 9

B check to make sure you and the child are in a safe place.

After making sure you're both safe, speak calmly and reassuringly to the child. Find out if the child is hurt or just scared. If the child has an injury you can take care of yourself, like a scraped knee, then follow proper first-aid procedures. Call 911 if the injury is life threatening. Then call the child's parents. Only do what you're trained to do.

page 12

A ask the child what she would like to play.

Be flexible. You might also want to dig deeper, and find out why the child doesn't want to play.

page 25

D stop playing and talk with the children.

It doesn't matter who started the fight. Let the children know that fighting is not allowed. Ask the children if they need help working things out. Decide whether it's best to continue the game or do something else.

page 26

D try to give both children equal attention.

You are a special person in the children's house. Both children will want your attention. Ask the 5-year-old to help you stack blocks with the 2-year-old.

Glossary

age-appropriate (AYJ uh-PRO-pree-uht)—being fit or right for a certain age

attention span (uh-TEN-shuhn SPAN)—the length of time someone can concentrate or stay interested

coordinated (koh-OR-duh-nay-ted)—the ability to control body movements

development (duh-VEHL-up-ment)—the growth of someone or something

hazard (HAZ-urd)—something that is dangerous

mature (muh-TYUR)—having reached full growth or development

reimburse (ree-ihm-BERS)—to pay back

responsibility (ri-spon-suh-BIL-uh-tee)—a duty or job

Read More

American Red Cross. *American Red Cross Babysitter's Training Handbook.* Yardley, Penn.: Staywell, 2008.

Babysitting Secrets: Everything You Need to Have a Successful Babysitting Business. San Francisco: Chronicle Books, 2012.

Bondy, Halley. *Don't Sit on the Baby!: The Ultimate Guide to Sane, Skilled, and Safe Babysitting.* San Francisco: Zest Books, 2012.

Internet Sites

FactHound offers a safe, fun way to find Internet sites related to this book. All of the sites on FactHound have been researched by our staff.

Here's all you do:

Visit *www.facthound.com*

Type in this code: 9781491407639

 Check out projects, games and lots more at **www.capstonekids.com**

Index